Your 13 Moon Month Journey

This is an undated journal.

You can begin your Moon Journey at any time of the year.

Just begin this book on any

NEW MOON

This Book Belongs To:

_____

Date Begun: _____

Visit our page
facebook.com/ SpiritualAwakeningPortal

Your 13 Moon Month Journey

"She has fought many wars, most internal. The ones that you battle alone, for this, she is remarkable. She is a survivor."
— **Nikki Rowe**

We are wild women. We are women that are moved by the ebb and flow of the waxing and waning of the moon.

No matter if you are young or an old crone, like myself, the moon calls to us. Our bodies are intrinsically entwined with the power of the moon's phases. This is why this journal was created. When you can tune into the beauty of the moon and align it to the beauty you have with in you , you can empower yourself to new heights.

We can see that the moon's energy effects all living things. So by tuning into and being more aware of the moon's cycles is a beautiful and empowering way way to foster self awareness and a deep connection to the planet around us.

I have created this Moon Journal to help guide you through the moon phases. Indigenous people were sensitive to the uniqueness of each moon phase, to point of naming them. We can become much more sensitive to the unique and different effects each phase has on our bodies and emotions?

It is a hope that this journal will guide you gently on a journey of self discovery by using questions and ritual tailored to work with the different phases of the moon to birth ideas, dreams, habits, and other facets of yourself that may have been hidden from you up to now.

These are only suggestions so please do not feel you MUST do it this way. You can use this as journal in any way you choose to. There are plenty of blank pages for your personal reflection, notes, drawings or whatever else happens when your pen meets the paper.

As you practice over the course of the year, it is our hope that you will open up a new portal of self examination that allows you to see your inner beauty so that you can learn to truly fall in love with yourself and all your power that you hold within.

"The moon is a loyal companion.
It never leaves. It's always there,
watching, steadfast, knowing us in our
light and dark moments, changing
forever just as we do. Every day it's a
different version of itself. Sometimes
weak and wan, sometimes strong and
full of light. The moon understands what
it means to be human.
Uncertain. Alone. Cratered by
imperfections."

— Tahereh Mafi, Shatter Me

13 Moons – 28 Days

All over the world, cultures and communities have mapped the moon cycle, which happens 13 times per year, in cycles of 28 days.

Most Women have their period every 28 days, this is why we are so connected to the Moon and her cycles. We are cycling with the cosmic power of

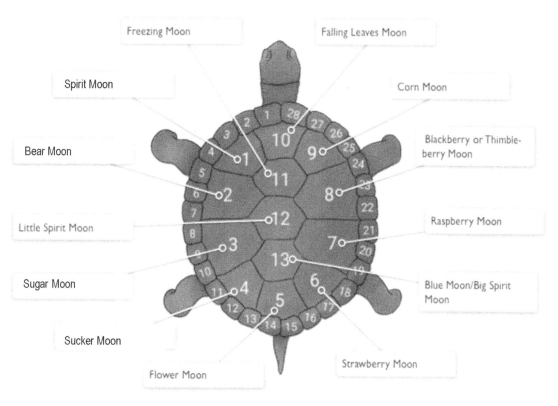

Kanawayhitowin. (n.d.). *Moon teachings.*
http://www.kanawayhitowin.ca/?page_id=214

From Moon Teachings

Thirteen Grandmother Moon Teachings
http://www.kanawayhitowin.ca/?page_id=214

January — Spirit Moon
The first moon of Creation is Spirit Moon, and is manifested through the Northern Lights. It is a time to honour the silence and realize our place within all of Great Mystery's creatures.

February — Bear Moon
The second moon of Creation is Bear Moon, when we honour the vision quest that it began in the fall. During this time, we discover how to see beyond reality and to communicate through energy rather than sound.

March — Sugar Moon
The third moon of Creation is Sugar Moon. As the maple sap begins to run, we learn of one of the main medicines given to the Anishnabe which balances our blood, and heals us. During this time, we are encouraged to balance our lives as we would our blood sugar levels, by using Divine Law.

April — Sucker Moon
The fourth moon of Creation is Sucker Moon, when sucker goes to the Spirit World in order to receive cleansing techniques for this world. When it returns to this realm, it purifies a path for the Spirits and cleanses all our water beings. During this time we can learn to become healed healers.

May — Flower Moon
The fifth moon of Creation is Flower Moon, where all plants display their Spirit sides for all the world to see. This life giving energy is one the most powerful healing medicines on Mother Earth. During this moon we are encouraged to explore our Spiritual essences.

June — Strawberry Moon
The sixth moon of Creation is Strawberry Moon. The medicine of the strawberry is reconciliation. It was during this moon cycle that communities usually held their annual feasts, welcoming everyone home, regardless of their differences over the past year, letting go of judgment and/or self-righteousness.

July — Raspberry Moon
The seventh moon of Creation is Raspberry Moon, when great changes begin. By learning gentleness and kindness, we may pass through the thorns of its bush and harvest its fruit, knowledge that will help in raising our families.

August — Thimbleberry Moon
The eighth moon of Creation is the Thimbleberry Moon, when we honour the Thimbleberry which produces an abundance of fruit once every three years. It was one of the first plants put on Mother Earth, and its purpose is to protect the Sacred Circle of Life by allowing us to recognize and understand the teachings that come from the Spirit World.

September — Corn Moon
The ninth moon of Creation is the Corn Moon, during which time we learn about the cycle of life. Each cob of corn has thirteen rows of multicoloured seeds which represent all the spirits waiting to begin their Earth Walk. These will be the future generations for whom we must prepare.

October — Falling Leaves Moon
The tenth moon of Creation is the Falling Leaves Moon, a time when Mother Earth is honoured with the grandest of colours. As all of Creation makes their offerings to her, we become aware of all the miracles of Creation before us and our spiritual energies are once again awakened.

November — Freezing Moon
The eleventh moon of Creation is the Freezing Moon, a time when the Star Nation is closest to us. As every creature being prepares for the coming fasting grounds, we are reminded to prepare ourselves for our spiritual path by learning the sacred teachings and songs that will sustain us.

December — Little Spirit Moon
The twelfth moon of Creation is the Little Spirit Moon, a time of healing. By receiving both vision of the spirits and good health, we may walk the Red Road with purest intentions, and we can share this most positive energy with our families and friends for the good of all.

Blue Moon Big Spirit Moon
The thirteenth moon of Creation is Big Spirit Moon. Its purpose is to purify us, and to heal all of Creation, a process which may take a three month long spiritual journey. During this time, we receive instructions on the healing powers of the universe and transform into our own vision of the truth.

Thirteen Grandmother Moon Teachings by Arlene Barry, from her series of compiled teachings "Kinoomaadiewinan Anishinaabe Bimaadinzinwin", Book Two, pages 17 and 18.

New Moon

Wiping the slate clean and setting new intentions

How Do You Feel?

_____

_____

_____

_____

_____

_____

_____

_____

_____

How do you wish to feel and Why?

_____

_____

_____

_____

_____

Do you believe you can achieve your goals?

_____

_____

_____

_____

_____

This New Moon I Intend:

_____

_____

I Am Grateful For

1. _____
2. _____
3. _____
4 _____
5. _____
6. _____
7. _____
8. _____
9. _____
10. _____

Notes:

I Begin Manifesting This Cycle

1. _____
2. _____
3. _____

People I Would Love To Help

1. _____
2. _____
3. _____

This or something better now manifests for
me in totally satisfying and harmonious
ways, for the highest good of all
concerned.

_____

_____

_____

_____

_____

_____

_____

First Quarter Moon

Date: _____

About 7 Days After New Moon

Working hard to realize your goals

How Do You Feel?

_____
_____
_____
_____
_____
_____
_____
_____
_____
_____

Are You Making Progress On Your New Moon Goals?

_____
_____
_____
_____
_____

How Can You Improve On Your Progress So Far?

_____
_____
_____
_____
_____

Full Moon

Manifesting your deepest intentions and desires

How Does This Full Moon Make You Feel Deep Inside?

_____
_____
_____
_____
_____
_____
_____
_____

We Are Halfway Through This Moon Cycle? Time To Dream BIGGER and Reach For The Stars. Visualize Your Completion of Your New Moon Goals

_____
_____
_____
_____
_____
_____
_____
_____
_____

This Full Moon I Release

_____

_____

My Limiting Beliefs

1. _____

2. _____

3. _____

4 _____

I am unique.

I have mission.

I have a calling.

I will fulfill my highest potential
and calling.

People I Forgive

1. _____

2. _____

3. _____

Things I Need To Let Go

1. _____

2. _____

3. _____

Notes:

_____

_____

_____

_____

_____

_____

_____

_____

_____

_____

Last Quarter Moon

About 7 Days After Full Moon

Releasing the bad energies and those things which aren't serving you

How Is Your Energy Level? Is Anything Draining You?

_____
_____
_____
_____
_____
_____
_____
_____
_____
_____

In This Last Phase Can You SEE Your Dream Manifest?

_____
_____
_____
_____
_____

How Can You Improve On Your Progress So Far?

_____
_____
_____
_____
_____

Reflections For This Moon Cycle

Moon

2

MOON PHASE
MORNING
EVENING

Color Code

Positive   Not Happy   Neutral

New Moon

Date: _____

Begins Lunar Cycle

Wiping the slate clean and setting new intentions

How Do You Feel?

_____
_____
_____
_____
_____
_____
_____
_____
_____

How do you wish to feel and Why?

_____
_____
_____
_____
_____

Do you believe you can achieve your goals?

_____
_____
_____
_____
_____

This New Moon I Intend:

_____

_____

I Am Grateful For

1. _____

2. _____

3. _____

4 _____

5. _____

6. _____

7. _____

8. _____

9. _____

10. _____

Notes:

I Begin Manifesting This Cycle

1. _____

2. _____

3. _____

People I Would Love To Help

1. _____

2. _____

3. _____

This or something better now manifests for me in totally satisfying and harmonious ways, for the highest good of all concerned.

_____

_____

_____

_____

_____

_____

First Quarter Moon

Date: _____

About 7 Days After New Moon

Working hard to realize your goals

How Do You Feel?

_____
_____
_____
_____
_____
_____
_____
_____
_____

Are You Making Progress On Your New Moon Goals?

_____
_____
_____
_____

How Can You Improve On Your Progress So Far?

_____
_____
_____
_____

Full Moon

Manifesting your deepest intentions and desires

How Does This Full Moon Make You Feel Deep Inside?

_____
_____
_____
_____
_____
_____
_____
_____
_____

We Are Halfway Through This Moon Cycle? Time To Dream BIGGER and Reach For The Stars. Visualize Your Completion of Your New Moon Goals

_____
_____
_____
_____
_____
_____
_____
_____
_____

This Full Moon I Release

_____

_____

My Limiting Beliefs

1. _____

2. _____

3. _____

4 _____

I am unique.

I have mission.

I have a calling.

I will fulfill my highest potential
and calling.

People I Forgive

1. _____

2. _____

3. _____

Things I Need To Let Go

1. _____

2. _____

3. _____

Notes:

_____

_____

_____

_____

_____

_____

_____

_____

_____

_____

Last Quarter Moon

Date: _____

Releasing the bad energies and those things which aren't serving you

How Is Your Energy Level? Is Anything Draining You?

_____
_____
_____
_____
_____
_____
_____
_____
_____
_____

In This Last Phase Can You SEE Your Dream Manifest?

_____
_____
_____
_____
_____

How Can You Improve On Your Progress So Far?

_____
_____
_____
_____
_____

Reflections For This Moon Cycle

Moon

3

MOON PHASE

MORNING

EVENING

1 2 3 4 5 6 7 8 9 10 11 12 13 14 15 16 17 18 19 20 21 22 23 24 25 26 27 28 29 30 31

Color Code

Positive   Not Happy   Neutral

New Moon

Wiping the slate clean and setting new intentions

How Do You Feel?

_____
_____
_____
_____
_____
_____
_____
_____
_____

How do you wish to feel and Why?

_____
_____
_____
_____
_____

Do you believe you can achieve your goals?

_____
_____
_____
_____
_____

This New Moon I Intend:

_____
_____

I Am Grateful For

1. _____
2. _____
3. _____
4 _____
5. _____
6. _____
7. _____
8. _____
9. _____
10. _____

Notes:

I Begin Manifesting This Cycle

1. _____
2. _____
3. _____

People I Would Love To Help

1. _____
2. _____
3. _____

This or something better now manifests for me in totally satisfying and harmonious ways, for the highest good of all concerned.

_____
_____
_____
_____
_____
_____
_____

First Quarter Moon

Date: _____

About 7 Days After New Moon

Working hard to realize your goals

How Do You Feel?

_____
_____
_____
_____
_____
_____
_____
_____
_____
_____

Are You Making Progress On Your New Moon Goals?

_____
_____
_____
_____

How Can You Improve On Your Progress So Far?

_____
_____
_____
_____
_____

Full Moon

About 14 Days After New Moon

Manifesting your deepest intentions and desires

How Does This Full Moon Make You Feel Deep Inside?

_____
_____
_____
_____
_____
_____
_____
_____
_____

We Are Halfway Through This Moon Cycle? Time To Dream BIGGER and Reach For The Stars. Visualize Your Completion of Your New Moon Goals

_____
_____
_____
_____
_____
_____
_____
_____
_____
_____

This Full Moon I Release

_____

_____

My Limiting Beliefs

1. _____

2. _____

3. _____

4 _____

I am unique.

I have mission.

I have a calling.

I will fulfill my highest potential
and calling.

Notes:

_____

_____

_____

_____

_____

_____

_____

_____

_____

People I Forgive

1. _____

2. _____

3. _____

Things I Need To Let Go

1. _____

2. _____

3. _____

Last Quarter Moon

Date: _____

Releasing the bad energies and those things which aren't serving you

How Is Your Energy Level? Is Anything Draining You?

_____
_____
_____
_____
_____
_____
_____
_____

In This Last Phase Can You SEE Your Dream Manifest?

_____
_____
_____
_____

How Can You Improve On Your Progress So Far?

_____
_____
_____
_____

Reflections For This Moon Cycle

Moon
4

MOON PHASE
MORNING
EVENING

1
2
3
4
5
6
7
8
9
10
11
12
13
14
15
16
17
18
19
20
21
22
23
24
25
26
27
28
29
30
31

Color Code

Positive   Not Happy   Neutral

New Moon

Wiping the slate clean and setting new intentions

How Do You Feel?

_____
_____
_____
_____
_____
_____
_____
_____
_____

How do you wish to feel and Why?

_____
_____
_____
_____
_____

Do you believe you can achieve your goals?

_____
_____
_____
_____
_____

This New Moon I Intend:

_____

_____

I Am Grateful For

1. _____

2. _____

3. _____

4 _____

5. _____

6. _____

7. _____

8. _____

9. _____

10. _____

Notes:

I Begin Manifesting This Cycle

1. _____

2. _____

3. _____

People I Would Love To Help

1. _____

2. _____

3. _____

This or something better now manifests for me in totally satisfying and harmonious ways, for the highest good of all concerned.

_____

_____

_____

_____

_____

_____

First Quarter Moon

About 7 Days After New Moon

Working hard to realize your goals

How Do You Feel?

_____
_____
_____
_____
_____
_____
_____
_____

Are You Making Progress On Your New Moon Goals?

_____
_____
_____
_____
_____

How Can You Improve On Your Progress So Far?

_____
_____
_____
_____
_____

Full Moon

Manifesting your deepest intentions and desires

How Does This Full Moon Make You Feel Deep Inside?

_____
_____
_____
_____
_____
_____
_____
_____
_____

We Are Halfway Through This Moon Cycle? Time To Dream BIGGER and Reach For The Stars. Visualize Your Completion of Your New Moon Goals

_____
_____
_____
_____
_____
_____
_____
_____
_____

This Full Moon I Release

_____
_____

My Limiting Beliefs

1. _____
2. _____
3. _____
4 _____

I am unique.
I have mission.
I have a calling.
I will fulfill my highest potential
and calling.

People I Forgive

1. _____
2. _____
3. _____

Things I Need To Let Go

1. _____
2. _____
3. _____

Notes:

_____
_____
_____
_____
_____
_____
_____
_____

Last Quarter Moon

Date: _____

Releasing the bad energies and those things which aren't serving you

How Is Your Energy Level? Is Anything Draining You?

_____
_____
_____
_____
_____
_____
_____
_____
_____
_____

In This Last Phase Can You SEE Your Dream Manifest?

_____
_____
_____
_____
_____

How Can You Improve On Your Progress So Far?

_____
_____
_____
_____
_____

Reflections For This Moon Cycle

Moon
5

MOON PHASE
MORNING
EVENING

Color Code

Positive   Not Happy   Neutral

"Wild woman are an unexplainable spark of life. They ooze freedom and seek awareness; they belong to nobody but themselves yet give a piece of who they are to everyone they meet.

If you have met one, hold on to her, she'll allow you into her chaos, but she'll also show you her magic." —Nikki Rowe

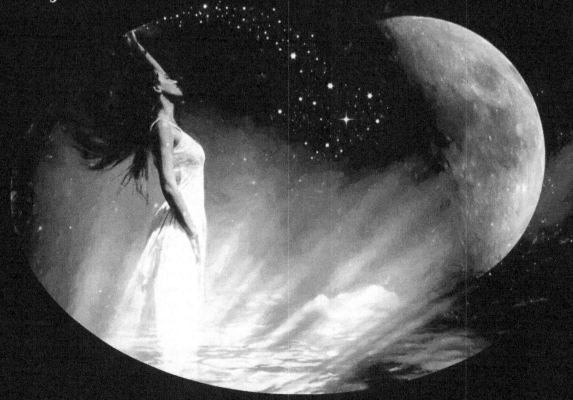

New Moon

Wiping the slate clean and setting new intentions

How Do You Feel?

_____
_____
_____
_____
_____
_____
_____
_____
_____

How do you wish to feel and Why?

_____
_____
_____
_____

Do you believe you can achieve your goals?

_____
_____
_____
_____
_____

This New Moon I Intend:

_____

_____

I Am Grateful For

1. _____

2. _____

3. _____

4 _____

5. _____

6. _____

7. _____

8. _____

9. _____

10. _____

Notes:

I Begin Manifesting This Cycle

1. _____

2. _____

3. _____

People I Would Love To Help

1. _____

2. _____

3. _____

This or something better now manifests for me in totally satisfying and harmonious ways, for the highest good of all concerned.

_____

_____

_____

_____

_____

_____

First Quarter Moon

About 7 Days After New Moon

Working hard to realize your goals

How Do You Feel?

_____
_____
_____
_____
_____
_____
_____
_____

Are You Making Progress On Your New Moon Goals?

_____
_____
_____
_____
_____

How Can You Improve On Your Progress So Far?

_____
_____
_____
_____
_____

Full Moon

Manifesting your deepest intentions and desires

How Does This Full Moon Make You Feel Deep Inside?

_____

_____

_____

_____

_____

_____

_____

_____

_____

We Are Halfway Through This Moon Cycle? Time To Dream BIGGER and Reach For The Stars. Visualize Your Completion of Your New Moon Goals

_____

_____

_____

_____

_____

_____

_____

_____

_____

This Full Moon I Release

_____

_____

My Limiting Beliefs

1. _____

2. _____

3. _____

4 _____

I am unique.

I have mission.

I have a calling.

I will fulfill my highest potential
and calling.

People I Forgive

1. _____

2. _____

3. _____

Things I Need To Let Go

1. _____

2. _____

3. _____

Notes:

_____

_____

_____

_____

_____

_____

_____

_____

_____

Last Quarter Moon

About 7 Days After Full Moon

Releasing the bad energies and those things which aren't serving you

How Is Your Energy Level? Is Anything Draining You?

_____

_____

_____

_____

_____

_____

_____

_____

_____

In This Last Phase Can You SEE Your Dream Manifest?

_____

_____

_____

_____

How Can You Improve On Your Progress So Far?

_____

_____

_____

_____

_____

Reflections For This Moon Cycle

Moon

6

MOON PHASE
MORNING
EVENING

Color Code

Positive   Not Happy   Neutral

New Moon

Wiping the slate clean and setting new intentions

How Do You Feel?

_____
_____
_____
_____
_____
_____
_____
_____
_____

How do you wish to feel and Why?

_____
_____
_____
_____
_____

Do you believe you can achieve your goals?

_____
_____
_____
_____
_____

82

This New Moon I Intend:

_____

_____

I Am Grateful For

1. _____

2. _____

3. _____

4. _____

5. _____

6. _____

7. _____

8. _____

9. _____

10. _____

Notes:

I Begin Manifesting This Cycle

1. _____

2. _____

3. _____

People I Would Love To Help

1. _____

2. _____

3. _____

This or something better now manifests for me in totally satisfying and harmonious ways, for the highest good of all concerned.

_____

_____

_____

_____

_____

_____

First Quarter Moon

About 7 Days After New Moon

Working hard to realize your goals

How Do You Feel?

_____
_____
_____
_____
_____
_____
_____
_____
_____
_____

Are You Making Progress On Your New Moon Goals?

_____
_____
_____
_____
_____

How Can You Improve On Your Progress So Far?

_____
_____
_____
_____
_____
_____

Full Moon

Manifesting your deepest intentions and desires

How Does This Full Moon Make You Feel Deep Inside?

_____
_____
_____
_____
_____
_____
_____
_____

We Are Halfway Through This Moon Cycle? Time To Dream BIGGER and Reach For The Stars. Visualize Your Completion of Your New Moon Goals

_____
_____
_____
_____
_____
_____
_____
_____

This Full Moon I Release

_____

_____

My Limiting Beliefs

1. _____

2. _____

3. _____

4 _____

I am unique.

I have mission.

I have a calling.

I will fulfill my highest potential

and calling.

People I Forgive

1. _____

2. _____

3. _____

Things I Need To Let Go

1. _____

2. _____

3. _____

Notes:

_____

_____

_____

_____

_____

_____

_____

_____

_____

_____

Last Quarter Moon

Releasing the bad energies and those things which aren't serving you

How Is Your Energy Level? Is Anything Draining You?

_____
_____
_____
_____
_____
_____
_____
_____
_____

In This Last Phase Can You SEE Your Dream Manifest?

_____
_____
_____
_____
_____

How Can You Improve On Your Progress So Far?

_____
_____
_____
_____
_____

Reflections For This Moon Cycle

MOON PHASE
MORNING
EVENING

Moon
7

Color Code

Positive   Not Happy   Neutral

New Moon

Wiping the slate clean and setting new intentions

How Do You Feel?

_____
_____
_____
_____
_____
_____
_____
_____
_____

How do you wish to feel and Why?

_____
_____
_____
_____
_____

Do you believe you can achieve your goals?

_____
_____
_____
_____
_____

This New Moon I Intend:

_____

_____

I Am Grateful For

1. _____

2. _____

3. _____

4 _____

5. _____

6. _____

7. _____

8. _____

9. _____

10. _____

Notes:

I Begin Manifesting This Cycle

1. _____

2. _____

3. _____

People I Would Love To Help

1. _____

2. _____

3. _____

This or something better now manifests for me in totally satisfying and harmonious ways, for the highest good of all concerned.

_____

_____

_____

_____

_____

_____

First Quarter Moon

Date: _____

About 7 Days After New Moon

Working hard to realize your goals

How Do You Feel?

_____
_____
_____
_____
_____
_____
_____
_____

Are You Making Progress On Your New Moon Goals?

_____
_____
_____
_____

How Can You Improve On Your Progress So Far?

_____
_____
_____
_____
_____

Full Moon

Manifesting your deepest intentions and desires

How Does This Full Moon Make You Feel Deep Inside?

_____
_____
_____
_____
_____
_____
_____
_____
_____

We Are Halfway Through This Moon Cycle? Time To Dream BIGGER and Reach For The Stars. Visualize Your Completion of Your New Moon Goals

_____
_____
_____
_____
_____
_____
_____
_____
_____
_____

This Full Moon I Release

_____

_____

My Limiting Beliefs

1. _____

2. _____

3. _____

4 _____

I am unique.
I have mission.
I have a calling.
I will fulfill my highest potential
and calling.

People I Forgive

1. _____

2. _____

3. _____

Things I Need To Let Go

1. _____

2. _____

3. _____

Notes:

_____

_____

_____

_____

_____

_____

_____

_____

_____

Last Quarter Moon

Date: _____

About 7 Days After Full Moon

Releasing the bad energies and those things which aren't serving you

How Is Your Energy Level? Is Anything Draining You?

_____
_____
_____
_____
_____
_____
_____
_____
_____

In This Last Phase Can You SEE Your Dream Manifest?

_____
_____
_____
_____
_____

How Can You Improve On Your Progress So Far?

_____
_____
_____
_____
_____

Reflections For This Moon Cycle

MOON PHASE
MORNING
EVENING

Moon
8

1 2 3 4 5 6 7 8 9 10 11 12 13 14 15 16 17 18 19 20 21 22 23 24 25 26 27 28 29 30 31

Color Code

Positive   Not Happy   Neutral

New Moon

Wiping the slate clean and setting new intentions

How Do You Feel?

_____
_____
_____
_____
_____
_____
_____
_____
_____
_____

How do you wish to feel and Why?

_____
_____
_____
_____
_____

Do you believe you can achieve your goals?

_____
_____
_____
_____
_____

This New Moon I Intend:

_____

_____

I Am Grateful For

1. _____

2. _____

3. _____

4. _____

5. _____

6. _____

7. _____

8. _____

9. _____

10. _____

Notes:

I Begin Manifesting This Cycle

1. _____

2. _____

3. _____

People I Would Love To Help

1. _____

2. _____

3. _____

This or something better now manifests for me in totally satisfying and harmonious ways, for the highest good of all concerned.

_____

_____

_____

_____

_____

_____

_____

First Quarter Moon

About 7 Days After New Moon

Working hard to realize your goals

How Do You Feel?

_____
_____
_____
_____
_____
_____
_____
_____
_____

Are You Making Progress On Your New Moon Goals?

_____
_____
_____
_____

How Can You Improve On Your Progress So Far?

_____
_____
_____
_____
_____

Full Moon

About 14 Days After New Moon

Manifesting your deepest intentions and desires

How Does This Full Moon Make You Feel Deep Inside?

_____
_____
_____
_____
_____
_____
_____
_____
_____
_____

We Are Halfway Through This Moon Cycle? Time To Dream BIGGER and Reach For The Stars. Visualize Your Completion of Your New Moon Goals

_____
_____
_____
_____
_____
_____
_____
_____
_____
_____
_____

This Full Moon I Release

_____

_____

My Limiting Beliefs

1. _____

2. _____

3. _____

4 _____

I am unique.

I have mission.

I have a calling.

I will fulfill my highest potential

and calling.

People I Forgive

1. _____

2. _____

3. _____

Things I Need To Let Go

1. _____

2. _____

3. _____

Notes:

_____

_____

_____

_____

_____

_____

_____

_____

_____

_____

Last Quarter Moon

Date: _____

Releasing the bad energies and those things which aren't serving you

How Is Your Energy Level? Is Anything Draining You?

_____
_____
_____
_____
_____
_____
_____
_____
_____

In This Last Phase Can You SEE Your Dream Manifest?

_____
_____
_____
_____
_____

How Can You Improve On Your Progress So Far?

_____
_____
_____
_____
_____

Reflections For This Moon Cycle

Moon
9

MOON PHASE
MORNING
EVENING

Color Code

Positive   Not Happy   Neutral

New Moon

Wiping the slate clean and setting new intentions

How Do You Feel?

_____

_____

_____

_____

_____

_____

_____

_____

_____

How do you wish to feel and Why?

_____

_____

_____

_____

_____

Do you believe you can achieve your goals?

_____

_____

_____

_____

_____

This New Moon I Intend:

_____

_____

I Am Grateful For

1. _____

2. _____

3. _____

4 _____

5. _____

6. _____

7. _____

8. _____

9. _____

10. _____

Notes:

I Begin Manifesting This Cycle

1. _____

2. _____

3. _____

People I Would Love To Help

1. _____

2. _____

3. _____

This or something better now manifests for me in totally satisfying and harmonious ways, for the highest good of all concerned.

_____

_____

_____

_____

_____

_____

_____

First Quarter Moon

About 7 Days After New Moon

Working hard to realize your goals

How Do You Feel?

_____
_____
_____
_____
_____
_____
_____
_____
_____
_____

Are You Making Progress On Your New Moon Goals?

_____
_____
_____
_____
_____

How Can You Improve On Your Progress So Far?

_____
_____
_____
_____
_____

Full Moon

Manifesting your deepest intentions and desires

How Does This Full Moon Make You Feel Deep Inside?

_____
_____
_____
_____
_____
_____
_____
_____
_____

We Are Halfway Through This Moon Cycle? Time To Dream BIGGER and Reach For The Stars. Visualize Your Completion of Your New Moon Goals

_____
_____
_____
_____
_____
_____
_____
_____
_____
_____

This Full Moon I Release

_____

_____

My Limiting Beliefs

1. _____

2. _____

3. _____

4 _____

I am unique.

I have mission.

I have a calling.

I will fulfill my highest potential
and calling.

People I Forgive

1. _____

2. _____

3. _____

Things I Need To Let Go

1. _____

2. _____

3. _____

Notes:

_____

_____

_____

_____

_____

_____

_____

_____

_____

Last Quarter Moon

Date: _____

About 7 Days After Full Moon

Releasing the bad energies and those things which aren't serving you

How Is Your Energy Level? Is Anything Draining You?

_____
_____
_____
_____
_____
_____
_____
_____
_____

In This Last Phase Can You SEE Your Dream Manifest?

_____
_____
_____
_____
_____

How Can You Improve On Your Progress So Far?

_____
_____
_____
_____
_____

Reflections For This Moon Cycle

Moon
10

MOON PHASE
MORNING
EVENING

Color Code

Positive   Not Happy   Neutral

New Moon

Wiping the slate clean and setting new intentions

How Do You Feel?

_____
_____
_____
_____
_____
_____
_____
_____
_____

How do you wish to feel and Why?

_____
_____
_____
_____
_____

Do you believe you can achieve your goals?

_____
_____
_____
_____
_____

This New Moon I Intend:

_____
_____
_____

I Am Grateful For

1. _____
2. _____
3. _____
4 _____
5. _____
6. _____
7. _____
8. _____
9. _____
10. _____

Notes:

I Begin Manifesting This Cycle

1. _____
2. _____
3. _____

People I Would Love To Help

1. _____
2. _____
3. _____

This or something better now manifests for me in totally satisfying and harmonious ways, for the highest good of all concerned.

_____
_____
_____
_____
_____
_____
_____

First Quarter Moon

Date: —————————

About 7 Days After New Moon

Working hard to realize your goals

How Do You Feel?

_____
_____
_____
_____
_____
_____
_____
_____

Are You Making Progress On Your New Moon Goals?

_____
_____
_____
_____
_____

How Can You Improve On Your Progress So Far?

_____
_____
_____
_____
_____

Full Moon

Manifesting your deepest intentions and desires

How Does This Full Moon Make You Feel Deep Inside?

_____
_____
_____
_____
_____
_____
_____
_____
_____

We Are Halfway Through This Moon Cycle? Time To Dream BIGGER and Reach For The Stars. Visualize Your Completion of Your New Moon Goals

_____
_____
_____
_____
_____
_____
_____
_____
_____
_____

This Full Moon I Release

_____

_____

My Limiting Beliefs

1. _____

2. _____

3. _____

4 _____

I am unique.
I have mission.
I have a calling.
I will fulfill my highest potential
and calling.

People I Forgive

1. _____

2. _____

3. _____

Things I Need To Let Go

1. _____

2. _____

3. _____

Notes:

_____

_____

_____

_____

_____

_____

_____

_____

_____

Last Quarter Moon

About 7 Days After Full Moon

Releasing the bad energies and those things which aren't serving you

How Is Your Energy Level? Is Anything Draining You?

_____
_____
_____
_____
_____
_____
_____
_____
_____

In This Last Phase Can You SEE Your Dream Manifest?

_____
_____
_____
_____
_____

How Can You Improve On Your Progress So Far?

_____
_____
_____
_____
_____

Reflections For This Moon Cycle

Moon

11

MOON PHASE
MORNING
EVENING

Color Code

Positive   Not Happy   Neutral

New Moon

Wiping the slate clean and setting new intentions

How Do You Feel?

_____
_____
_____
_____
_____
_____
_____
_____
_____

How do you wish to feel and Why?

_____
_____
_____
_____
_____

Do you believe you can achieve your goals?

_____
_____
_____
_____
_____

This New Moon I Intend:

_____

_____

I Am Grateful For

1. _____

2. _____

3. _____

4 _____

5. _____

6. _____

7. _____

8. _____

9. _____

10. _____

Notes:

I Begin Manifesting This Cycle

1. _____

2. _____

3. _____

People I Would Love To Help

1. _____

2. _____

3. _____

This or something better now manifests for me in totally satisfying and harmonious ways, for the highest good of all concerned.

_____

_____

_____

_____

_____

_____

First Quarter Moon

Date: _____

About 7 Days After New Moon

Working hard to realize your goals

How Do You Feel?

_____
_____
_____
_____
_____
_____
_____
_____
_____

Are You Making Progress On Your New Moon Goals?

_____
_____
_____
_____

How Can You Improve On Your Progress So Far?

_____
_____
_____
_____
_____

Full Moon

About 14 Days After New Moon

Manifesting your deepest intentions and desires

How Does This Full Moon Make You Feel Deep Inside?

_____
_____
_____
_____
_____
_____
_____
_____
_____

We Are Halfway Through This Moon Cycle? Time To Dream BIGGER and Reach For The Stars. Visualize Your Completion of Your New Moon Goals

_____
_____
_____
_____
_____
_____
_____
_____
_____

This Full Moon I Release

_____

_____

My Limiting Beliefs

1. _____

2. _____

3. _____

4 _____

I am unique.

I have mission.

I have a calling.

I will fulfill my highest potential
and calling.

People I Forgive

1. _____

2. _____

3. _____

Things I Need To Let Go

1. _____

2. _____

3. _____

Notes:

_____

_____

_____

_____

_____

_____

_____

_____

_____

Last Quarter Moon

About 7 Days After Full Moon

Releasing the bad energies and those things which aren't serving you

How Is Your Energy Level? Is Anything Draining You?

_____

_____

_____

_____

_____

_____

_____

_____

_____

_____

In This Last Phase Can You SEE Your Dream Manifest?

_____

_____

_____

_____

_____

How Can You Improve On Your Progress So Far?

_____

_____

_____

_____

_____

Reflections For This Moon Cycle

Moon

12

MOON PHASE

MORNING

EVENING

Color Code

Positive   Not Happy   Neutral

"Practice listening to your intuition, your inner voice; ask questions; be curious; see what you see; hear what you hear; and then act upon what you know to be true. These intuitive powers were given to your soul at birth."

― Clarissa Pinkola Estés,

New Moon

Date: _____

Begins Lunar Cycle

Wiping the slate clean and setting new intentions

How Do You Feel?

_____
_____
_____
_____
_____
_____
_____
_____
_____

How do you wish to feel and Why?

_____
_____
_____
_____
_____

Do you believe you can achieve your goals?

_____
_____
_____
_____
_____

This New Moon I Intend:

_____
_____

I Am Grateful For

1. _____
2. _____
3. _____
4 _____
5. _____
6. _____
7. _____
8. _____
9. _____
10. _____

Notes:

I Begin Manifesting This Cycle

1. _____
2. _____
3. _____

People I Would Love To Help

1. _____
2. _____
3. _____

This or something better now manifests for me in totally satisfying and harmonious ways, for the highest good of all concerned.

_____
_____
_____
_____
_____
_____

First Quarter Moon

About 7 Days After New Moon

Working hard to realize your goals

How Do You Feel?

_____
_____
_____
_____
_____
_____
_____
_____
_____
_____

Are You Making Progress On Your New Moon Goals?

_____
_____
_____
_____
_____

How Can You Improve On Your Progress So Far?

_____
_____
_____
_____
_____

Full Moon

About 14 Days After New Moon

Manifesting your deepest intentions and desires

How Does This Full Moon Make You Feel Deep Inside?

_____
_____
_____
_____
_____
_____
_____
_____
_____
_____

We Are Halfway Through This Moon Cycle? Time To Dream BIGGER and Reach For The Stars. Visualize Your Completion of Your New Moon Goals

_____
_____
_____
_____
_____
_____
_____
_____
_____
_____
_____

This Full Moon I Release

_____

_____

My Limiting Beliefs

1. _____

2. _____

3. _____

4 _____

I am unique.
I have mission.
I have a calling.
I will fulfill my highest potential
and calling.

Notes:

_____

_____

_____

_____

_____

_____

_____

_____

People I Forgive

1. _____

2. _____

3. _____

Things I Need To Let Go

1. _____

2. _____

3. _____

Last Quarter Moon

Date: _____

Releasing the bad energies and those things which aren't serving you

How Is Your Energy Level? Is Anything Draining You?

_____

_____

_____

_____

_____

_____

_____

_____

_____

In This Last Phase Can You SEE Your Dream Manifest?

_____

_____

_____

_____

_____

How Can You Improve On Your Progress So Far?

_____

_____

_____

_____

_____

Reflections For This Moon Cycle

Moon
13

MOON PHASE
MORNING
EVENING

Color Code

Positive   Not Happy   Neutral

New Moon

Wiping the slate clean and setting new intentions

How Do You Feel?

_____

_____

_____

_____

_____

_____

_____

_____

_____

How do you wish to feel and Why?

_____

_____

_____

_____

Do you believe you can achieve your goals?

_____

_____

_____

_____

_____

This New Moon I Intend:

_____

_____

I Am Grateful For

1. _____

2. _____

3. _____

4 _____

5. _____

6. _____

7. _____

8. _____

9. _____

10. _____

Notes:

I Begin Manifesting This Cycle

1. _____

2. _____

3. _____

People I Would Love To Help

1. _____

2. _____

3. _____

This or something better now manifests for me in totally satisfying and harmonious ways, for the highest good of all concerned.

_____

_____

_____

_____

_____

_____

_____

First Quarter Moon

Date: _____

Working hard to realize your goals

How Do You Feel?

_____
_____
_____
_____
_____
_____
_____
_____

Are You Making Progress On Your New Moon Goals?

_____
_____
_____
_____

How Can You Improve On Your Progress So Far?

_____
_____
_____
_____

Full Moon

Manifesting your deepest intentions and desires

How Does This Full Moon Make You Feel Deep Inside?

_____
_____
_____
_____
_____
_____
_____
_____

We Are Halfway Through This Moon Cycle? Time To Dream BIGGER and Reach For The Stars. Visualize Your Completion of Your New Moon Goals

_____
_____
_____
_____
_____
_____
_____
_____
_____

This Full Moon I Release

_____
_____

My Limiting Beliefs

1. _____
2. _____
3. _____
4 _____

I am unique.
I have mission.
I have a calling.
I will fulfill my highest potential
and calling.

People I Forgive

1. _____
2. _____
3. _____

Things I Need To Let Go

1. _____
2. _____
3. _____

Notes:

_____
_____
_____
_____
_____
_____
_____
_____

Last Quarter Moon

D a t e : _____

Releasing the bad energies and those things which aren't serving you

How Is Your Energy Level? Is Anything Draining You?

_____
_____
_____
_____
_____
_____
_____
_____
_____
_____

In This Last Phase Can You SEE Your Dream Manifest?

_____
_____
_____
_____
_____

How Can You Improve On Your Progress So Far?

_____
_____
_____
_____
_____

Reflections For This Moon Cycle

We hope you
enjoyed your journey around
the annual moon phases.

Please leave a review if this book
helped you. Your positive vibrations
are greatly appreciated.

Visit our page
facebook.com/ SpiritualAwakeningPortal

Made in the USA
Las Vegas, NV
08 September 2022

54898902R00105